DAO DE JING

Laozi's Timeless Wisdom

a new translation by
Dian Duchin Reed

Humanitas Press
Soquel, California

Copyright © 2016 by Dian Duchin Reed

ISBN: 0692742824
ISBN-13: 978-0692742822
Library of Congress Control Number: 2016945404
Humanitas Press
3145 Center Street, Soquel, CA 95073, USA

Cover: snail shell, photo taken by the author
www.DianDuchinReed.com

This book is dedicated to

Mary Kaplan Duchin and Christopher Reed

Acknowledgements

Individual poems from this collection have appeared, sometimes in different versions, in the following literary journals:

Salamander (chapters 6 and 7)
Poetry East (chapters 10, 11, and 12)
Parabola Magazine's Facebook page (chapter 15)
Lalitamba (chapters 39, 51, 54, 55, and 56)
Ezra: an online journal of translation (chapters 1–5)

With Gratitude

The author would like to thank the following people:

Professor Charles Bell, whose intensive Chinese-language class made this translation possible

Simu Kuo, whose instruction in taiji quan has resulted in three decades of daily practice

Carl Abbott, whose Center For Taoist Thought And Fellowship has provided the fellowship of like-minded seekers for the last several years

Contents

Introduction

There's a reason that Laozi's *Dao De Jing* is one of the world's most translated and popular pieces of literature. Not only does each translator produce a new understanding, so does each reader. That's because the path, the Dao, is as personal as it is universal.

This new translation from the Chinese retains the beauty and nuances of the original Chinese text, while remaining as true to its meaning as possible. The goal was to make a clear translation, while allowing mystery to continue to curl through each chapter like fragrant incense. The subject matter—human nature and the workings of the universe—is as relevant to the present as it was to the past, as it will be to the future. Though written twenty-five hundred years ago, these eighty-one short chapters can still change a reader's life.

It's worth noting that the third-person-singular pronoun in Chinese is gender-neutral. Using the conventional default of their era, the earliest English translators chose the words *he* and *him*. Subsequent interpretations were often based on these early translations, inadvertently maintaining the original bias. A modern translation of the *Dao De Jing* calls for less convention and more awareness, starting with an awareness of the text's high regard for the feminine.

Philosophy, religion, mysticism, spirituality... these are simply words, of which the *Dao De Jing* is rightly cautious. Beginning with the first chapter, it is obvious that the Dao, the mysterious path, is something that can be pointed at, but not pinned down. The Dao is as fluid as a butterfly flapping its dazzling wings. Pinning it down is the beginning of labels with words, and the end of movement.

Perspective is key, but, as Laozi says, *There's no way for a fish to step back from its lake.* Still, the *Dao De Jing* manages to provide a startling look at life from outside of our daily comfort zone, giving insight on such topics as how to live, relationships with others, attaining goals, war and peace. Far from meeting preconceptions, the text is meant to surprise the reader, leading to a reperception, reevaluation, and reconsideration of what has until then been taken for granted.

No need to leave home to travel down this path. Those who are flexible and kind, those who do what's only natural, will find it as close as a heartbeat, as far-reaching as the end of the universe.

—Dian Duchin Reed

1 Crooked Cup of Awe

A path that can take you places
is not a continuing path.
A name that can describe things
is not an eternal description.

There's no way to describe
the beginning of the universe.
Description is the source of all things.

Forget about desire
if you want to see wonders,
or indulge in desire
if you'd rather admire distinctions.

Both awe and water pour from
the same spout, yet how different
they seem after they're out.
You might call their similarity
a dark mystery.

Darkness as darkness
as doorway to mystery.

2 Go Ahead

Go ahead—whistle at beauty;
she'll spin around to show you
ugliness stuck to her back.

Pin a medal on goodness,
and evil will start oozing out
through the puncture holes.

All because nothing
keeps giving birth to
its mother something.

The hard-to-win prize
and my easily caught eyes
depend on each other.

The longest marriage
and the briefest flame
define each other.

Yesterday and tomorrow
make time for each other.

That's why those who know
find fulfillment without effort,
leaving silence unshivered.

All things arise,
none decline the invitation.

Best to live without controlling,
act without expecting,
perform well without dwelling on it.

Only those who don't claim things
will never lose them.

3 Nothing Doing

No longer on the lookout for the worthy and gifted,
we're free from envy.

No longer on the lookout for the precious and rare,
we're free from theft.

Listen, the desirable can look after itself;
the heart would rather be at ease
than always at attention, and wisdom—

doesn't it?—comes down to this:
to empty the mind and fill the stomach,
to soften ambition and strengthen bones.

Before we know it, we're without
boast or thirst, and best of all
we're stabbing no one with our sharp wit.

Oh
we do nothing.
And the universe takes care of itself.

4 Never Mind

The universe is an empty bottle in constant use

one that never drains or fills

unfathomable source

from which all things pour

It takes the edge off sharpness

smoothes out the kinks

softens the razzle-dazzle

makes every one of us from the same atomic dust

Unimaginably deep unbelievably clear but never
mind

it seems to exist anyway

we have no idea

where it came from

it's nobody's baby

born even before the ultimate ancestor

5 Words

The universe couldn't care less
when the downed tree crumbles
into mushrooms and worms

and if you're wise, you won't care either
when age tosses beauty aside.

Isn't the universe a vast black hat?
Empty but full of magic.

The more you reach in, the more you pull out.

Words, words, words—
such a fortune wasted.

Better to burrow quietly into the center.

6 Usefulness

The mystery of the valley
is never still. Let's call this mystery
female. And her door—let's call it
the root of the universe.
She's soft, but seems to survive.
Her usefulness has nothing
to do with hard work.

7 The Secret

How long the universe lives!
Even the Earth exists
for a long, long time.

Because their lives are not
how they identify themselves,
they can live forever.

That's why the way to last
is to put yourself last,
not first

and the way to survive
is to keep yourself
out of the running.

To avoid your own end,
avoid the usual way of passing
from this to that.

That's the secret.

8 Why Water

Better to be as kind as water,
which benefits all and argues with none.
Water gets along with everyone,
oblivious to hate or slander.
That's why water flows
close to the path.

Be kind to the earth, your heart
a deep pool of compassion,
your words friendly and truthful.

Kind control is unselfish,
and kind work is skillful.
The only way not to argue
is to act kind,
so dismiss discontent.

9 Directions

Sure, grasping will fill you,
but not with your self,

and reckoning will keep you sharp,
but may not always keep you safe.

The treasure goes to the seeker;
the owner has already lost it.

To those who love wealth: arrogance
To those who lose themselves: misfortune
To those who achieve success: retreat

Reality lies in this direction.

10 Call It Kindness

Now that you've embraced
your rapturous life, of course
you're reluctant to leave it!

A whirlpool of energy, you might try
yielding like a baby. And stop
mopping up mystery—it's not a stain!

You claim that you care about
the health of the world, but do you act
like someone who loves to live here?

Now, here's how to open
the doorway to heaven:
softly, tenderly.

It's clear and plain
and all around you—
surely you can't miss it.

In the meantime, creation
keeps churning you out, keeps
raising you like corn or cattle.

It gives you life,
but has no expectations.

Gives you action,
but without attachment.

Gives you growth,
but plans no harvest.

Ah. Might as well call it
mysterious kindness.

11 The Value of Nothing Much

A bunch of spokes
    or a simple hub
is nothing much,
    but fit them together
to make a wheel,
    and it can be useful.

Water alone
    or a bit of clay
is nothing much,
    but knead them together
to make a bowl,
    and it too can be useful.

Cutting out a lone door
    or a single window
is nothing much,
    but cut them both out
to make a room,
    and, yes, it can be useful.

This is just to say that
    good things are waiting
even if you start with
    nothing much.

12 Hunting for Hints

Call it cloud,
and the eye stops seeing.

Call it trill,
and the ear can't hear.

Call it yam,
and the mouth won't taste it.

This hunting for hints
and rushing to conclusions—
it's enough to drive you crazy!

Not to mention the harm
of wanting something
so badly.

If you're wise,
you'll rely on the belly
and not the mind's eye.

Grasp what's really here;
cast away those mirages.

13 As If

Pelt me with praise or insults
and I'll be startled,

but my own yearning and worries—
I'm used to their inner percolation.

When praise suddenly hits me,
of course I'm alarmed! Same
with the flinging of failure.

What's so different about yearning and worries?

Only I can have worries—
why else do I exist?
If I didn't have an I, who would have
all these worries?

And yearning…well,
yearning creates the world.
No yearning, no world.
No world, no yearning.

The fondness I once felt for my self
I now apply to the whole world.

As if I'm entrusted with everything.

14 The Singular Era

I'm looking   but not seeing,
listening   but not really hearing,
grabbing   but just not getting it.

These are some of the things people say
when they're wasting time,
or hoping for more,
or living a life of denial—

three good ways to avoid awareness
that add up to a single muddle.
Drifting along like this, nothing
is gained; paying attention,
nothing is hidden.

Mist mists, dawn dawns—
clearly, what's happening here
beggars description.
Return to the state
of no things.

You might call this fading
a waste of what the world has
to offer. You might call it faint
as a whisper, blurred
as a rain-soaked note.

No face appears, no back
in sight. To manage
the present, observe the ancient
beginning. You might call this
the singular era of truth.

15 How to Succeed

From the beginning, the successful
have focused on understanding
wisdom, wonder, and mystery.
They were deep, but didn't know it.

Because they really didn't know,
they were obliged to act in a way
that fit every situation perfectly.

Oh, how carefree!
To experience winter as a river
or a meadow would, respecting everything.

How marvelous!
To know that fixed appearances can dissolve—
like ice, ready to be freed into water.

How kind!
Life as plain and simple and ample,
life as a channeling valley.

And, ah, how wholly
natural! Life as deep
and dense and muddled.

How can you be clouded, yet quiet?
By slowly clearing things up.
How can you be safe, yet aroused?
By gently bringing things forth.

Maintain this art. Don't wish for more.
It's true—forget about filling yourself;
instead find shelter in every fresh success.

16 Emptiness

The best description of emptiness:
serious stillness.
Of course, every single thing that exists

rises side by side with me,
and all of us will return
to our original state.

This return—that's what it means to be still.
That's the original state.
A good name for this return is awareness,

because all will be clear. Lack of awareness
is absurd and a terrible way to grow.
Awareness always fits the situation,

which is why it's fair. What's fair is best,
and what's best is natural,
which is the way the universe exists.

As a result, the universe
lasts a long time. My personal end
does not endanger the universe.

17 How to Know It

From top to bottom,
the greatest are those
who are aware of its existence.

Next come those
who are as intimate
as they are eminent.

Next, those who fear it,
and, finally, those
who ridicule it.

In this case, to have faith
is not excessive;
in this case, to have no faith

is simply sad!
Its precious words
accomplish good deeds

and satisfy responsibilities.
Every single person
calls it *my nature*.

18 No Difference

Even if morality is left behind,
charity and kindness continue on.

When wisdom and knowledge appear,
countless falsehoods follow.

Whether or not one's kin are kind,
there will still be love and duty.

It makes no difference

if the nation's thinking is mixed up
and muddled; honest politicians exist.

19 What's Desirable

When the holy disappears
and knowledge is abandoned,
   people benefit many times over.

When kindness disappears
and charity is abandoned,
   people return to affectionate duty.

When the skillful disappears
and the favorable is abandoned,
   theft and deceit do not occur.

These three scenarios are not usually
taken into consideration
   as much as they should be,

and that's because bringing about
what's desirable
   depends on

seeing what's simple,
cherishing what's plain,
   and lacking what's selfish.

Best to have
modest
   desires.

20 The Disappearance of Knowledge

If knowledge disappears, don't be too concerned.
Instead, consider the distance between
knowledge and mutual flattery. Or
between success and mutual slander.

When it comes to people, what they don't fear,
they certainly don't respect. It's absurd!
They're not in the center! Many of them
thrive splendidly, as if they're enjoying

the world's greatest jail, or as if
their *joie de vivre* were displayed on a table.
Only I have cast my anchor! This is a sign,
but it's not as good as a baby; it's not even

a tired, worn-out child! It's more like
not really belonging. Only I seem lost,
even though there are more than enough
of all kinds of people.

It's only me here.
A person with a center!
Powered by the slow and dull!
Others wear their brightness openly,

while I prefer the dimness of dusk. Others
observe and inspect everything around them,
while I keep myself
to myself.

There are all kinds of people,
including my own humble self—
or, at the moment,
my stubborn self.

I may be unusual
in relation to others,
but I'm as bountiful as a banquet
to the one who conceived us all.

21 The Entrance

The only way to enter the path
is to engage in kindness.

The path becomes
the outside world,

only indistinct, and faint.

Faint! Indistinct! It hits
the mark—it appears to exist.

Indistinct! Faint! It takes
the prize—it's the outside world.

Elegant! Profound! It's in
the process of being refined,

its refinement completely unmistakable.

It's all right to have faith.

From the beginning until this moment,
its place is not apart from us,

because many experience it right now.
Right now, why should I make use

of this knowledge anyway?
Because of this very moment.

22 Empty Words

Bent yet intact, crooked but straight.
Hollow then full, shabby then new.
Lost but gained, lavish yet abashed.

According to those who know,
it's best to embrace all of it,
every single thing.

Seeing doesn't mean
perceiving. Being doesn't mean
being obvious.

Boasting doesn't bring about
accomplishment. Conceit
doesn't bring about expertise.

Only those who don't struggle
can have it all. There's nothing
that can argue with them.

From the beginning these people
have been called bent yet intact—
how empty these words are!

Intact indeed, yet
gathered together
with every single thing.

23 Indescribable

To admire words is natural.

After all, it's not the end of *morning*
when the wind gusts,
and *day* doesn't die
in a sudden rain.

This is what words act like:
the universe.

And yet the universe doesn't have
infinite ability;
how much more so when it comes
to people!

Consider the matter of existence—
it's indescribable.
Kindness or goodness—indescribable.
Failure—indescribable too.

Existence, kindness or goodness,
failure—all have no problem
permitting their own indescribability.

In this case, to have faith
is not excessive.
Why not have faith?

24 Leftovers

People on tiptoe don't stand straight;
those who ride don't walk.

People who see are not perceptive;
those who are right aren't praised.

Boasters accomplish nothing,
and the egotistical are no experts.

Yes, such people dwell along the path;
you might call them last night's leftovers.

From the look of things,
perhaps this is slander.

There's a reason it's a path
and not a dwelling.

25 Not Dangerous

Before the universe appeared, things were aimless, muddled. Silent! Empty! Alone and unchanging. All around, but not dangerous. I certainly think it all began this way. I don't know how to describe it; the best I can do is to call it a path. What I mean is that—because of its reputation—I should call it important. What I call important is whatever passes. What passes is a name for what's far away. What's far away is a name for what returns. That's why the path is important. The universe is important. Our planet is important. And we too, we are important as well. In this domain, all four are important—although people are in a singular position among them. People are a sample of our planet. The planet is a sample of the universe. The universe is a sample of the path. And the path...the path is a sample of what's natural.

26 The Importance of the Unimportant

What's important is the origin
of the unimportant. What's calm
becomes Mr. Road Rage.

For the wise person, no day ends
without considering what's important
and what's not.

At any rate, there is joy
in observing while at ease, pleasure
in remaining at a distance.

It's no help when a person
takes extreme advantage, yet believes
that the whole world is unimportant.

Unimportant, yet the origin
of a mistake. Mr. Road Rage,
yet Mr. Mistake.

27 Blueprint for Wisdom

Behave well, and never mind hiding your tracks.
Speak well, and forget about blaming your flaws.
Evaluate well, and there's no need to keep count.

Close the door well
and skip the lock—
the door can't open.

Tie the string well
and don't bother about the knot—
the string can't be untied.

According to those who know,
always acting well saves people,
so don't abandon people.

Always acting well also saves material,
so don't throw things away.
This is called *following the blueprint for wisdom*.

The person who is well-disposed to others
is an example
for those who are not inclined to be kind,

and the person who is not well-disposed
is a resource
for those who are.

Such an example is not valued,
and such a resource is not enjoyed…
still,

great wisdom has its fans.
This is called
wanting what's wonderful.

28 Nothing Exceptional

Aware of the strong and defending the tender,
you serve the world as a stream.
For such a stream,
constant kindness isn't far.

> *Go back, return to being a baby.*

Aware of the bright and defending the shady,
you serve the world as an example.
For such an example,
constant kindness is no mistake.

> *Go back, return to being nothing exceptional.*

Aware of the honored and defending the disgraced,
you serve the world as a valley.
For such a valley,
constant kindness is ample.

> *Go back, return to being simple.*

Simplicity, loosely used, becomes a tool
for those who know,
who then become those who control:
great control with nothing severed.

29 Mystery

As I see it,
the problem with
wants and wishes
is that they're not about to stop.

The whole world is a mystery—
a tool certainly not suited to serve.
Serving, mystery
defeats any plan, makes it fail.

Mystery is efficient, or maybe it's laissez-faire.
Maybe it whispers, or perhaps it blares.
Maybe it compels, or else it helps.
Maybe it fills, or maybe it razes.

Those who know
say to do without
what's extreme
                extravagant
                        exceptional.

30 Returns

Use the path to assist people.
Don't use power to compel them.
Such a venture pays good returns.

For example, how can being in difficulties
support life? Propagate force,
and an ominous harvest will certainly follow.

Being kind yields fruit, that's all there is to it.

Forcible gain, attacking, stubbornness,
arrogance, pride, and boasting—
refrain from these and reap the results.

Strength exists, but never
on the path. For a long time now,
not on the path.

31 War or Peace

An excellent army doesn't bring luck. More likely,
it's a tool to be feared. Therefore, walk the path
of kindness, don't stop to punish. Worthy people
live according to the precious rules of peace.
Those who crave power value the rules of war.

Power is an ominous tool, the wrong tool
for worthy people. If they use it, it's because
they have no choice. Not caring for fame or gain,
they perform better and emerge victorious,
but not pleased with themselves.

Those who are pleased with themselves
are happy to kill people. Happy to kill people,
they certainly can't be allowed to fulfill
their ambitions and take over the world.

A lucky venture values peace. An ill-fated venture—
one that involves casualties—values violence.

Those who love the rules of peace,
but must lead an army, do better to lead the army
according to the rules of a funeral service.

That is to say, a funeral service also deals with
dead people, and the grief and wailing of many.
An army's victory is really a funeral.

32 Short and Sweet

The path has never been described.

Though it's simple and short, surely there is no one
in the world who can follow it all the way.

If moguls and magnates could last on it,
doubtless the rest of us would want to come along.

All of creation would seem as sweet as nectar.

There is no one person who makes it happen; each
of us is equally likely. This begins to describe it.

And while it's also true that the description
already exists, that knowledge will end.

It's certainly not dangerous, when
knowledge ends. For example, the path

covers the entire planet, just as the valley
channels the river, and the river seeks the sea.

33 Flex

To know about people	takes wisdom.
To know about yourself	is perceptive.
To defeat people	takes strength.
To surpass yourself	takes vigor.
To be content	is to be rich.
To make yourself shape up	takes willpower.
To eliminate mistakes	takes a long time.
To live with rigor	is nearly rigor mortis.

34 The Extent of the Path

The path is wide and vast!
Clearly it extends to all sides.
Everything relies on it
in order to enter the world,
and not depart.

It performs these admirable deeds,
        but isn't celebrated.
It clothes and raises everyone,
        but doesn't control a soul.
It has no needs, is never greedy—
        its fame is oh-so-small!
Though taking care of everything,
        the path owns...nothing.

Yet it's a big-name attraction,
because it's the whole and not the parts.
It's prodigious. That's why
it can accomplish such great feats.

35 Music and Cakes, Bread and Circuses

Stick to appearances, and the whole world spins.
It turns, yet does no harm, so peaceful and calm.
It's amusing! Its music and cakes
might entice you to stay
       instead of passing through.

The path, though, is blah in the mouth—
no taste at all. And no smell. Take a look at it—
there's nothing there to see or touch.
Listen to it—you won't hear a sound.
Eat it, drink it, try to use it—
       it's nowhere to be found.

36 Step Back

If you want to breathe in,
of course you have to open up.

If you want to weaken,
you have to make an effort.

If you want to clean out,
first you have to be inspired.

If you want to get it,
it's clear that you must give it.

You might call this understanding
         beyond understanding.

It's better to be weak and flexible
than firm and forceful.

There's no way for a fish
to step back from its lake.

A nation may be a helpful tool,
but it reveals nothing about people.

37 Wishing for a Description

The path never does a thing,
but nothing is left undone.

If moguls and magnates
could last on it,
it would certainly change
the rest of us.

Transformed, we'd want
to write about it.

I would suppress
that wish
because the path's description
should not be simple,

although it seems to me
that a description
that is not simple
would also be nothing
to wish for.

Don't wish to write about it
in order to be calmly settled.

The whole world is certainly
ready to pin it down.

38 Clearing Confusion

Better kindness is not always kindness,
    but that's what kindness is about.
Lesser kindness is constantly kind,
    and that's why it's not really kindness.

Better kindness lets things take their own course,
    and doesn't think about it.
Lesser kindness also does nothing,
    but stops to think about it anyway.

Better compassion acts, and doesn't think about it.
Better generosity acts, but stops to think about it.
Better courtesy acts, but people don't use it properly.
Then, throwing up their arms in dismay,
they toss it away.

What does this mean?
Deviate from the path,
    and kindness follows.
Deviate from kindness,
    and compassion follows.
Deviate from compassion,
    and generosity follows.
Deviate from generosity,
    and courtesy follows. (Courteous people
are so loyal and sincere
    as to be unkind.)

And so confusion prevails.

People who knew the path
used to flower with magnificence
as well as foolishness.
These people of character
resided in their large generosity,
and didn't dwell on their small unkindness.
They resided in their fruitful reality,
and didn't dwell on their flowery magnificence.

Now you know which to choose
and which to abandon.

39 Like Jade

In the past, all was at ease—

sky	because it was clear
earth	because it was tranquil
soul	because it was nimble
valleys	because they were full
living things	because they grew
powerful people	because they were dedicated

Wholeness was the result. If things were otherwise,
the results would probably differ—

sky	would split off
earth	would be a wasteland
soul	would call it a day
valleys	would be drained
living things	would perish
the powerful	would be overthrown

To avoid these catastrophes,
what's precious should use what's common
as a foundation,
and the people at the top should see those
at the bottom
as a base.

Yes, the mighty should honor
the lonely, abandoned, and hungry,
but it's now considered wrong to use the humble
as a starting place. Wrong…?
Those who don't have eminence merit it most.

Jade longs for nothing. A chunk of jade
is as good as a fine jade necklace;
a necklace is as good as a rock.

40 Return

Return
> is the movement of the path.

Weakness
> is what the path uses.

> Everything in the world appears here out of abundance.

> Abundance appears out of emptiness.

41 Clarity

Hearing about the path,
the best travelers go and walk it.
Average travelers who hear about it
tend to hold onto it as if it could be lost.
The worst kind of travelers find it ludicrous,

though not laughing doesn't mean
you believe in it. The truth is, when you try
to talk about the path clearly, it appears
to be hidden. When you step onto it,
it feels like returning. It's as seamless

as kindness, which at its best
is like a valley, empty but full
of potential. In describing the path,
clarity would be an insult, its out-
and-out kindness seemingly insufficient.

Really, to urge kindness doesn't seem right,
and to question it is like a betrayal.
Its whereabouts are so wide that no place
is bypassed, its capacity so great
that it lasts all day and into the night.

Its sound is so deep that it resonates like hope,
its appearance so sizable that it has no shape.
No description fits the hidden path,
yet it alone is kind. Borrow it for a while.
More than that, make it last.

42 Dynamics

The path brings about the universe.
The universe leads to duality. Duality gives birth to
many things, and the many turn into the infinite.

All of these things hold the secret and tote the overt,
a blend that produces dynamic energy.

There are people who fear being lonely or hungry,
but the powerful should laud those who lack.

In other words, some things do damage as well as
bring benefit, and others help as well as harm.

No one is wholly self-made or self-taught.
What makes a bridge powerful is not pride;
such a bridge is uncrossable.

Just as I am making others,
they are making me.

43 (Don't Tell Anyone)

Everyone in the world dashes back and forth
between fully flexible and completely unyielding,
and yet there's nothing to agree with,
no particular place to be. That's how I know
it's helpful to let things take their own course.

(Don't tell anyone about it. Better
let things take their own course.)

Everyone would like to accomplish this.

44 Contentment

How others know you
and how you experience yourself—
which is really you?

How you experience yourself
and what you own—
which can be excessive?

Contentment
and loss—
which is the problem?

Exactly.

That's why what you care about most
must cost a lot

and amassing to excess
must foster loss.

To be content is no disgrace.
To know when to stop is no threat.

In this way, you can prosper
for a long time.

45 All Right

The highly successful seem imperfect,
though this need not mean defeated.

The totally full seem cleaned out,
though this need not mean depleted.

The most upstanding look crooked,
the most artful appear awkward,
the loudest contenders sound hesitant.

Heated is better than cold,
and calm is better than burning.
Be clear and calm, and all will be right.

46 Enough

When everyone took to the path,
horses roamed, and fertilized fields with manure.
Now no one's on the path,
and towns raise war horses instead of food.

Nothing brings greater disaster
than not being satisfied with enough.
Nothing is more to blame
than the desire for gain.

Therefore,
be content with enough,
though enough
so often
bleeds into excess.

47 What Remains

No need to go out the door
to be mindful of the world.

No need to peer through windows
to see the right way to act.

The more you go out, remote and distant,
the more you know what's missing.

That's why those in the know
don't go anywhere but remain aware

of what's not visible, yet apparent.
Not seeing, they perceive.

Not making things happen,
they get results.

48 Subtraction

Every day you learn,
you add something.

Every day you walk the path,
you subtract something.

Subtract and keep subtracting
in order to let things
go their own way.

Leave things alone;
don't impose meaning.

To get what you want,
never get involved.
To be occupied
with what you want
is not enough to get it.

49 Getting It

Those who know
don't have endless intentions. They treat
other people's intentions as their own.

Kindness is good,
so I am kind to the person who is kind
and also to the person who is not.

Kindness is true,
so I trust the person who is truthful
and also the person who is not.

Those who know
are getting everything. Why? Because
the whole world is their sole intention.

Other people
are always paying attention
to what their eyes and ears tell them.

Those who know
are always concentrating
on the outcome.

50 Concealing Fame

Birth concurs with death—
of those being born,
only a few retain emptiness;
of those who are dying,
only a few remain unencumbered.

And of the living
there are also only a few
who continue to act
when in imminent danger.
How can this be?

Because they live
to give life
to kindness.

Conceal the fame of your kindness,
and you'll conserve your life.

Travel all over, meet no fierce beasts.
Enter the army, need no armor or guns.
You're open to spine or horn,
to claw or talon,
to knife-sharp blade.
How is this possible?

Because nothing
about you
is in imminent danger.

51 No Need

The path brings things to life,
kindness raises them,

the world shapes them,
and outward appearances result,

so of course all things respect the path
and consider kindness precious,

not because they must,
but because it's only natural, for the fact is,

the path conceives them, and kindness grows them,
rears them, brings them up, shelters

and stuns them, looks after them
and overwhelms them, and even though

the path engenders, it doesn't possess,
and even though kindness does deeds,

it has no needs, no,
it tends its herds, yet never harvests—

which is why it's called
mysterious kindness.

52 Practice, Practice, Practice

Think about it—for the universe to begin,
it must have been conceived. Since the universe
is a *fait accompli*, study its origin
to understand what's emerged,
and once you're aware of what's arisen,
resume your observation of the origin.

Your own end doesn't endanger this venture.

Stop up its changes and shut its door—
your personal sabotage will never get the job done.
Free up its changes and assist its operations—
all in all, your personal aid won't help.

To see it as small is called perception.

To defend its softness is called force.

Use only what it has to offer,
and keep returning to your perception of it.
Forget about deleting your personal disasters.
That's right, call this your constant practice.

53 Seriously

If I took what I know seriously,
I would walk on the wide path
and only act with respect.

Though the great path runs smooth
and safe, people keep stumbling
down shadowy byways—

Those in charge become estranged,
as weeds fill the fields
and warehouses empty.

Stuffed with food and drink,
with wealth and assets, these high-
fashion swashbucklers find life a bore.

Sure, call it praising
plunder. Nothing
like the path!

54 Using What's Here

The experts at setting things up
will not be left behind. The experts
at cherishing will not fade away.
Those who come after
will thank them forever.

Construct your life of kindness,
and be constant. Build a family of kindness,
and abide. Cultivate a hometown of kindness,
and exist forever. Make a nation of kindness,
and be inexhaustible. Create a world
of kindness, and be all-embracing.

So use your own life to define what
life suggests. Use your family to mean
family. Use your hometown to signify
birthplace. Use your country
as the concept of *nation*. Use your world
to represent a *living planet*.

What do I use
to know the world correctly?
I use what's here,
I use it now.

55 Harmony

Sucking in kindness
supplies more flavor
than what newborn babies get to drink.

Those who drink kindness
perceive kindness, not
noxious insects with vicious bites,
savage beasts with fearful claws,
plundering birds ominous as storms.

Babies have weak bones and soft muscles,
but a strong grip on things.
They know nothing yet about the parts
that join to make a whole—male/female,
hill/valley, key/keyhole—yet all babies
grow most proficiently.

The result of babies' howling
at the end of the day is not hoarseness,
but harmony and peace. To know
such harmony is said to be common
for babies. To know what's common
is said to be perceptive. Being born
brings benefits you've got to call successful.

When the mind issues instructions
for breathing, it makes an effort
instead of letting the body do what it does
naturally. Such a mind is strong, but stubborn,

which means it's not on the path.
It will be spending a long time
not on the path.

56 More Words

Those who are aware
are not talking about it.
Putting things into words
is not awareness.

Those who are aware
dampen their vigor and dispel confusion.
They reconcile their brightness
with the world of dust and dirt.

Yes, the words for this are
mysterious oneness. That's why
they certainly don't have to be
anything, but may be your intimate,

or else your most distant relation.
They're doing you good, or else
they're causing you trouble. Perhaps
they're valuable, perhaps insignificant.

In the end, they make
the whole world precious.

57 Stay Calm

Govern a nation with justice,
wield an army with surprising maneuvers,
but gain the whole world with non-involvement.
How do I know? I'll tell you.

Too many restrictions make people think
they're missing something. Too many sharp wits
make the nation dull and apathetic. Too much
cunning increases the world's surprise.

Clearly, rules make thieves more wily.
That's why those who know
realize *when I don't act,*
people transform themselves.

When I stay calm, people do
what's just. When I'm not involved,
people feel abundant. When I long
for nothing, people find life simple.

58 Shining, Not Stunning

When government keeps silent,
people are honest.
When government probes,
people make themselves scarce.

Disaster happens,
and happiness relies on it.
When happiness comes,
disaster bides its time.

Who knows life's ultimate state?
It's not about what's proper.
What's proper comes round as peculiar.
Goodness comes round as evil.

No wonder everyone's always confused.

The ones who know
know how to take part
without cutting anything off.

They're honest, but not brutally so;
confident, but not willful;
shining, but not stunning.

59 Repeat After Me

To govern people and serve nature,
        nothing beats living small.

Living small is called
        adapting beforehand.

Adapting beforehand is called
        the repeated accumulation of kindness.

With the repeated accumulation of kindness,
        nothing is impossible.

When nothing is impossible,
        no one knows life's limits.

No one knows life's limits,
        yet the nation exists.

The nation exists, conceived like the rest of us,
        but developing over a longer time.

Yes, this is called
        deep roots and a strong foundation.

A long life, and a long time
        to regard the path.

60 Not Exactly Magic

Managing a large nation
is like cooking a tiny delicacy;
best to approach every endeavor with kindness.
Such craftiness is not magic—
or, no, that's not exactly right,
it's more that such magic will not harm people.
Wait, that's not it either,
more that wise managers
will not harm those they manage—
neither of them will harm the other,
because kindness gathers people together.

61 Fitting Together

The large nation spills into the lesser one,
and she becomes his tender partner.

Because she is peaceful, she is superior to him;
because she is peaceful,
she assumes the lower position.

Being inferior, the large nation
takes the smaller one;
being lower, the smaller one is taken.

A nation can be inferior either
because it takes, or because it is taken.

The bigger one simply wants to continue
controlling people. The smaller one
only wants to help people.
Both of them get what they want.

How fitting that the larger one
should be inferior.

62 Insurance

The path is a mystery to everyone—
it's a treasure to the kind,
and insurance to the unkind.

Pleasing speech may be respected in public places,
and good behavior may enhance relationships,
but why leave behind those who are unkind?

Not even a powerful person's most expensive jade
or the fleetest team of horses
is as good as traveling on the path.

What makes this path so valuable?
To be kind is to be on the path, and to be unkind
is forgivable, so the path is precious to all.

63 Simplicity

Simply do, never mind about performing.
Simply engage, never mind about difficulties.
Simply taste, and forget about naming the flavor.

Forget big and small,
or too much this, too little that—
just repay blame with kindness.

Approach the difficult as if it were simple;
attain the large by dealing with details.
Certainly, all difficult problems
grow from simple ones,
just as all large problems grow from trifles.

Those who know advise taking nothing as important.
That way you can accomplish important things.

It's clear that reckless promises
inspire little confidence.
What seems too easy must turn into trouble.
According to those who know, problems persist;
so, in the end, never mind about problems.

64 Natural Action

Those who are calm find it easy to persevere.
Those who aren't focused on an outcome
find it easy to plan.
That which is crisp finds it easy to get soggy.
That which is tiny finds it easy to get mislaid.
These results are implied before they exist,
so they can be dealt with before confusion sets in.

A massive tree starts out as an air-blown seed.
A lofty building rises from a pile of dirt.
The longest hike begins when a foot
descends two inches.

Those who act willfully are defeated;
those who take charge fail.
Don't act, and there'll be no failure.
Don't take charge, and there'll be no mistake.

So often, people nearly succeed, then give up.
Finish as carefully as you started,
and forget about failure.

Best to wish for no desires,
for nothing rare or valuable.

Best to learn no knowledge
parroted by too many people.

Best to assist all people and things
to fulfill their nature,
without presuming to act.

65 Deception

It used to be that experts on the path
didn't use their skill publicly.
They did this in order to deceive.

People who know too much are difficult to manage,
so governing the nation by means of knowledge
entails deceit. To bring the nation happiness,
don't use knowledge to govern it.

Be aware of these two options,
and let them be your guide.
Always.

That's right, this is mysterious kindness.
As close as your heartbeat, as remote
as the end of the universe! The world
as we know it shows both sides.

As a result, the deepest well-being.

66 Kind Control

The ocean can control the drainage of many valleys,
but—being kind—it positions itself lower.
That's why it's in control.
Exactly so, say those who know—

If you want to be higher than other people,
you must speak as if you were lower.
If you want to be first among people,
you must put yourself last.

Be in a superior position,
but don't let people attach importance to it.
Take first place,
but don't make people feel uneasy.

Indeed, make everyone happy to promote you,
not be fed up with you.
Don't strive for power,
and no one in the world can dispute it.

67 Like Nothing Else

Everyone calls my path great.
It's like nothing else they know.
This path alone is great,
which is why it seems unique.

Really, if it were like anything else,
it would have become trifling a long time ago.

I have three jewels that I hold and preserve:
kindness, simple living, and reticence
to occupy a top position.

Using kindness, I can be courageous.
Living simply, I can be ample.
Being reticent, I can develop my talent.

These days, people give up kindness,
        but remain bold;
abandon simple living,
        yet expect abundance;
refuse reticence,
        and elbow their way to the front.
Stubborn indeed!

Those who are kind prevail and remain strong.
It's in the nature of things
to help and protect those who are kind.

68 Extraordinary

The best combatant is not fierce;
the first-rate fighter is not enraged—

which is to say that the way to win
is to remain unruffled.
The best manager is therefore humble.

Kind is another word for those who don't argue.
Powerful is another word for those who manage
others.

Extraordinary is a word for the joining of the two:
a time-honored, natural match.

69 The Good Fight

Those who are forced to fight say,
I never feel like an owner, but act like a guest.
I prefer to fall back a foot than advance an inch.

Really, they're revealing the way to
get somewhere without moving a leg,
throw into confusion without lifting an arm,
cast off a threat without resistance,
and take charge without violence.

There is no greater disaster than
reckless opposition. Through such rashness,
I almost lost what I treasure most.

The only good fight
is the war against violence.
Conquerors gain nothing
but grief and sorrow.

70 To Clarify

What I say is very easy to understand
and equally easy to do,
but nobody gets it, and nobody does it.

Words are limited by their implications,
actions by the force of habit.

The only reason no one grasps it
is because I don't either.

It's the rare person who understands me,
but what I have to say is precious.

Right. Though those who know
dress drably, a jewel adorns their heart.

71 The Problem

Best to know
that you don't know.

Not knowing this
is a problem.

Only those who are troubled
by this problem

have no problem.
Those who know

are not troubled
because their problem

is a problem
that they know about.

They alone—sick of this defect—
have nothing wrong with them.

72 About Power

People don't respect authority,
not until its power knocks them down.

No point denouncing their home-lives,
or getting fed up with their work-lives.
Just don't detest them,
because they're really not detestable.

Here's some advice about power
from those who know—

Be aware of yourself,
but don't promote yourself.
Be fond of yourself,
but don't imagine yourself precious.

Get rid of that, and
take this.

73 Nature's Web

Bravery that's brazen
means a fight to the death.

Bravery that dares no one
leads to staying alive.

> Both kinds of bravery
> may either help or harm.

Hatred, shame, and fear exist.
What's the reason?

According to those who know,
problems occur in spite of everything.

> Nature's way is not to fight,
> yet it succeeds.

Without speaking,
it gives the best response.

It rallies none, but receives all.
It's on the path, with a perfect plan.

> Nature's web is vast and its threads are fine,
> but nothing escapes it.

74 Fear of Dying

People don't respect death.
How can you make them dread dying?

Now, if they always feared death,
they would act in surprising ways.

I ought to observe such people, but
who dares to threaten another with death?

Generally, certain people are designated
to kill others. To act like one of them

is like passing yourself off
as a skilled wood-worker.

Would-be wood-workers only hope
their hands survive the attempt.

75 Nothing Special

When people go hungry,
it's because administrators
charge too much for food.

When people are hard to manage,
it's because of administrators
with potential.

When people disregard death,
it's because they're intent
on a bountiful life.

That's why these things happen.

Truly worthy people
consider life nothing special,
rather than precious.

76 The Benefit of Weakness

At birth, we're clearly weak and delicate.
It's death that turns us firm and unyielding.

Grasses and trees also start out flexible and fragile;
they dry and stiffen when they die.

That's why those who are strong
follow death,

and the weak and delicate
follow life.

Strength of arms usually loses.
The unbending tree often snaps.

The powerful stay low,
while the weak rise high.

77 Presents

Nature's path acts like a stretched bow,
pulling down what's high and lifting what's low.
What's excess decreases; what's lacking fills up.

The human path differs,
depleting those without enough,
letting the well-off stockpile the surplus.

Who can have extra and make a present of it
to the rest of the world?
Only those on the path,

because those who know
act like nature, without attachment.
They perform these admirable deeds,

but don't dwell on them.
They don't want to appear virtuous.
Heretical for a human.

78 The Correct Words

There's nothing as delicate and weak as water,
but to fall upon the firm and unyielding
nothing could be better than water,
which holds on to nothing, so amiable and simple.

Soft and supple is better than firm and strong.
The weak and inferior is superior to the powerful.
There's no one around who isn't aware of this,
and no one who can behave like this.

According to those who know,
the person who's humiliated by everyone
is the person who should manage everyone.

The person considered unsuccessful by everyone
is the person who's best, the strongest of all.
The correct words are the opposite words.

79 An Unorthodox Treaty

When people come to terms after intense hostility,
some blame will remain.

Because peace is a good thing,
those who know

honor an unorthodox treaty
that doesn't blame others.

Kindness enforces such a treaty.
Unkindness enforces perpetuation of blame.

Nature's path—though impersonal—
always plays a part in the ungrudging person.

80 In the Country of Contentment

It's a small country with few people.

Say there are a hundred different devices,
but no one uses them.
Say the people take death seriously,
and don't avoid the issue by moving house.

Maybe there are boats and cars,
but no one cares to travel.
If there are guns or armor,
no one cares to set them out.

Suppose the people continue the art
of tying knots—cross knot, ring hitch,
mystic knot—using them to decorate,
commemorate, and meditate.

They're fortunate with their food
and pleased with their clothes,
safe in their houses
and happy with their habits.

They're so close to their neighboring nations
that they can hear each other's dogs barking.
Still, they grow old and die, not needing
to compare or compete with any others.

81 The Power of Not

Faithful speech is not beautiful.
Beautiful speech is not faithful.

Kind people don't argue.
Those who argue aren't kind.

Awareness is not erudition.
Erudition is not awareness.

Those who know
don't accumulate much.

The more one thinks,
the more there is to think about.

The more one gives of oneself,
the greater the result.

Nature's path does good,
not harm.

The path of those who know
suits the purpose, but doesn't strive.

About the Author

Dian Duchin Reed was educated at the University of Chicago and New York University. She has won the Mary Lonnberg Smith Award in Poetry, a Sundberg Family grant for literary criticism, and the Mel Tuohey Award for writing excellence.

She has worked as a photojournalist (with articles and photographs in such magazines as *American Forests*, *National Geographic World*, and *Garden Design*) and a technical writer (for companies like Becton Dickinson and Johnson & Johnson).

Her recent poems and essays have appeared in *North American Review*, *Prairie Schooner*, *Nimrod International Journal*, *Poetry East*, *Poet Lore*, *The Nation*, and many other journals. Her chapbook, *Medusa Discovers Styling Gel*, was published by Finishing Line Press in December 2009.

She lives and writes within walking distance of the Monterey Bay National Marine Sanctuary.